RECORD BREAKERS

ANIMAL KINGDOM

DAVID JEFFERIS

RAINTREE
STECK-VAUGHN
PUBLISHERS

A Harcourt Company

Austin   New York

Published by Raintree Steck-Vaughn Publishers, an imprint of Steck-Vaughn Company.

Library of Congress Cataloging-in-Publication Data is available upon request

ISBN 0-7398-6321-5

Acknowledgments
We wish to thank the following individuals and organizations for their assistance and for supplying material from their collections:
Alpha Archive, Liz and Tony Bomford, Fred Bruemmer, Jane Burton, John Cancalosi, Bruce Coleman Collection, Corbis Images, Johnny Johnson, Janos Jurka, Richard Kolar, Ben Osborne, Sam Osolinski, Oxford Scientific Films, Jeffrey L Rotman, Rick Price, Kim Taylor, Terra Forma Globes, Jim Watt, Staffan Widstrand, Norbert Wu.

Diagrams by Gavin Page
Project modelling by
Emily Stapleton-Jefferis
Educational advisor Julie Stapleton

We have checked the records in this book but new ones are often added.

Printed in Taiwan. Bound in the United States.

1 2 3 4 5 6 7 8 9 0 07
06 05 04 03 02

▲ The grizzly brown bear is the most common bear in North America. A full-grown adult can weigh over 882 pounds (400 kg). The even bigger Alaska brown bear can weigh up to 1,764 pounds (800 kg).

On the cover: The lion is Africa's biggest wild cat. Adult males weigh more than 440 pounds (200 kg).

CONTENTS

World of Animals 4

Animal Movers 6

In the Air 8

Underwater Life 10

Animal Senses 12

Mealtime 14

Colors and Coats 16

Animal Homes 18

Longest Journeys 20

Life Spans 22

Extreme Survival 24

Animal Records 26

Animal Words 28

Animal Projects 30

Index 32

🐕 LOOK FOR THE ANIMAL SYMBOL

Look for the dog logo in boxes like this.
Here you will find extra facts and records.

WORLD OF ANIMALS

Our planet overflows with animal life—on land, in the air, and in the oceans. Scientists have studied nearly two million kinds of animal, and there are still others.

▲ There are over 250,000 kinds of beetle, more than any other insect. Beetles live almost everywhere, except in the oceans and icy polar areas.

▼ An adult male African elephant can grow nearly 13 feet (4m) high. He eats up to 770 pounds (350 kg) of food every day.

The smallest living creatures are tiny things called protists, most of which are far smaller than this period.

At the other end of the scale, the largest animal on our planet is the huge blue whale, which can grow to more than 33 yards (30 m) long.

The biggest land animal is the African elephant. The heaviest one ever weighed over 12 tons.

▼ A giraffe's long neck helps make it the tallest land animal, at about 20 feet (6 m) high.

▶ There are over 37,000 kinds of spider. The biggest is the goliath tarantula, which has a leg-span of up to 11 inches (28 cm). The smallest is the patu marplesi of Western Samoa, with a leg-span of .02 inch (0.43 mm)!

🐾 **MEGA WEB**

Not all spiders make webs, but thousands of tiny money spiders made the biggest web ever seen. It was found covering the whole playing field of a school at Kineton in Great Britain.

Tarantulas have very hairy legs.

Even though a giraffe's neck is long, it has only seven bones, the same as a human!

ANIMAL MOVERS

▲ The kangaroo is the world's fastest-hopping animal. Its huge back legs allow it to hop along at speeds of 40 mph (65 km/h).

▼ The cheetah from Africa is the fastest land animal. It can chase after prey at speeds of up to 62 mph (100 km/h).

Walking, leaping, hopping, swimming, and flapping are just a few ways animals get around.

The fastest animals are birds. Some birds can fly over 100 mph (160 km/h) in level flight. The fastest fish is the sailfish. It has been timed at speeds above 62 mph (100 km/h). On land, the cheetah holds the speed record.

▲ Some grasshoppers can leap 26 feet (8 m), which would equal a human jumping 656 feet (200 m)!

▲ The huge-finned sailfish has been timed at a speed of 67 mph (109 km/h). The biggest measured sailfish weighed 141 pounds (64 kg).

The cockroach is thought to be the fastest land insect. It has been timed scuttling along at nearly 3 mph (5 km/h). The dragonfly is the speediest flying insect. It can fly at speeds of 37 mph (60 km/h).

Cheetahs can run at top speed for only a short time.

🐕 AMAZING MOVEMENTS

Water Jet A cuttlefish squirts water back through a nozzle when it wants to move fast. The jet's force pushes it forward.

Hanging On The gecko lizard has special foot pads that can grip slippery surfaces. Using these pads, a gecko can climb walls and hang upside down on a ceiling!

Loopy Legs The looper caterpillar has two sets of legs, one at each end of its body. It curls its body in a loop and digs in with its back legs, while the front ones stretch ahead. Then the back legs catch up again for the next step.

Fastest Snake The black mamba can wriggle along at 12 mph (20 km/h).

▲ Hummingbirds are the smallest of all birds. They are the only birds that can fly backward and hover. This one is hovering by a flower to sip its sweet nectar.

IN THE AIR

There are more than 100,000 kinds of butterfly and moth.

The first flying creatures were insects, millions of years ago. Today the skies are filled with all kinds of flying animals.

The smallest flying insect is a kind of mini-wasp called the fairy fly. It is just .0008 inch (0.02 mm) long, small enough to squeeze through the eye of a needle. Compared to this, the biggest butterfly is a giant. An adult Queen Alexandra's birdwing of New Guinea has a wingspan of up to 11 inches (28 cm).

The smallest bird is the bee hummingbird. It is named for the noise made by its fast-beating wings, which flap 50 or more beats a *second*! The biggest bird of prey is the South American condor, which can weigh 26 pounds (12 kg). Flightless ostriches are much heavier, weighing up to 330 pounds (150 kg).

🐕 BIRD FACTS

Tiny Bird The smallest hummingbird weighs less than .01 ounce (2 g). Even the biggest hummingbird is less than 11 inches (27 cm) long and weighs only about .10 ounce (20 g).

Rarest Bird The last wild Brazilian Spix's macaw disappeared in 2000. People are trying to breed them from a

few still living in zoos.

Big Egg New Zealand's kiwi has the biggest egg compared to an adult bird. At more than 16 ounces (450 g), a kiwi egg weighs nearly 25 percent as much as its mother!

Owls' ears are hidden behind feathery tufts.

Quiet Killer The owl is a good hunter at night. It has soft-edged wing feathers that give almost silent flight, just right for closing in on unwary prey.

Peregrine falcon folds its wings when diving for prey—the dive is called a stoop.

Birds of prey, called raptors, have a sharp hooked beak.

▲ The peregrine falcon can reach more than 186 mph (300 km/h) in a dive, making it the fastest of all birds.

▶ Swans have more feathers than any other bird. An adult swan has about 25,000 feathers. Some 20,000 very fine feathers grow on the head and neck.

UNDERWATER LIFE

▲ Seahorses are thought to be the slowest fish. At full speed, a seahorse moves only about 10 inches (26 cm) per minute.

Water covers more than 70 percent of the planet's surface. Living in rivers, lakes, seas, and oceans are more than 24,000 kinds of fish.

The smallest fish is the tiny dwarf goby, which measures less than half an inch long. The biggest fish is the 39-foot (12-m)-long whale shark. Even though it is so big, it is not a vicious hunter. Instead, it is a gentle giant that cruises along with its mouth open, scooping up small creatures from the water.

The great white shark is considered the deadliest of all sharks. It has razor-sharp teeth and jaws that can rip off a 100-pound (45-kg) chunk of flesh in just one bite.

The biggest animal in the sea is the blue whale. It is an air-breathing mammal, not a fish. The huge creature feeds on tiny shrimplike sea creatures called krill. An adult blue whale can weigh 165 tons or more, so its appetite for 4 tons of krill every day is not too surprising!

▲ The blue whale is the largest animal that has ever lived. Even giant dinosaurs were not as big!

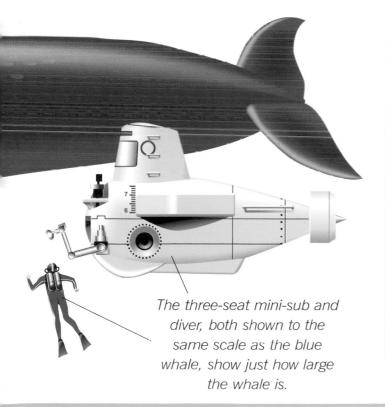

▲ The whale shark is not usually a danger to humans, but one did swallow a Japanese photographer by accident. The whale shark spat him out quickly, and he escaped with only scratches and bruises!

The three-seat mini-sub and diver, both shown to the same scale as the blue whale, show just how large the whale is.

🐕 FISHY FACTS

Deep Down The brotulid fish lives more than 5 miles (8 km) below the ocean's surface, where there is no light and the water pressure would crush you flat.

Big Eyes The giant squid has the largest eyes in the animal kingdom. They can be more than 1 foot (40 cm) across in an adult.

Killer Creature The stonefish of the Indian Ocean is the world's most poisonous fish.

ANIMAL SENSES

Animals experience the world around them and communicate with other animals by using their senses.

Bats have an amazing "super-sense." They send out high-pitched squeaks as they fly and can hear echoes that bounce back from solid objects, such as tree branches or the flying insects they eat. Dolphins also use high-pitched clicking sounds to get an idea of what's in nearby water.

Many animals call loudly to attract mates. Tropical cicadas can be heard nearly .5 miles (400 m) away. The loudest bird is thought to be the kakapo parrot from New Zealand; the male's deep call carries 4 miles (7 km)!

▲ Bats are the best night-fliers of all. They use "echolocation," which is a sense that allows them to find their way in the dark using sound instead of light. Here a bat hangs up to rest.

🐾 DANCE OF THE BEES

When a bee finds nectar, it can communicate this to other bees by making special dancing motions.

A bee dancing in a circle is showing that a source of nectar is not too far away. The bee can then wag its tail while running back and forth. This shows distance—the fewer runs, the farther away the nectar.

The bee can show which way to go by using the Sun as a compass. It can line up its tail to point out direction.

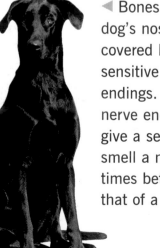

◄ Bones in a dog's nose are covered by many sensitive nerve endings. These nerve endings give a sense of smell a million times better than that of a human.

▶ Night-flying moths are the insect world's champion sniffers. Males have feathery antennas that pick up the scent of a female up to 6 miles (10 km) away.

▼ A polar bear's sense of smell is so good that the bear can smell the rotting flesh of a dead seal 19 miles (30 km) away.

A polar bear's diet includes seal, walrus, and fish.

MEALTIME

For many animals, life is short. It's kill or be killed by creatures bigger and faster than yourself. The top killers are carnivores, hunters that eat flesh.

▲ The world's fussiest eater is probably the koala from Australia. It lives on just one thing, eucalyptus tree leaves.

Some animals have to eat all the time. The smallest mammal, the tiny pygmy shrew, is one of them. It hunts for insects for 2–3 hours, has a rest, then looks for more food. If it doesn't eat for just one day, it will starve.

However, most animals can eat far less often than shrews. For example, a great white shark can survive for several weeks on one good-sized fish supper.

An adult locust is about 1.5–2.5 inches (4–6 cm) long.

◄ The desert locust is a large grasshopper that lives in parts of Africa, the Middle East, and India. When locusts swarm they become the most destructive insect in the world. Even a small swarm of 50 million locusts can destroy huge fields of crops, enough to feed 500 people.

▼ There are 41 kinds of wild dog, and the timber wolf is the biggest. These wolves hunt in a group or pack, working as a team to bring down big animals such as deer or caribou.

🐕 HUNTING IN PACKS

Fish Herders Despite their name, killer whales belong to the dolphin family. They are ferocious hunters and work together in groups. One trick they use is herding fish to shallow waters. Once the fish are all in one area, the killer whales take turns gobbling up the trapped fish without having to chase them.

Pack Cat Lions are the only wild cats that hunt in a pack. Females do most of the hunting, but they do share their catch with males and cubs.

Hunting Dog Along with wolves, dog hyenas are the best pack hunters. Hyenas make a kill on more than half their hunts.

A full-grown male weighs up to 176 pounds (80 kg).

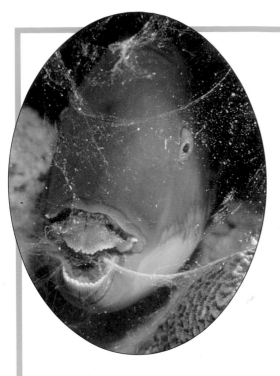

ANIMAL HOMES

Many animals build their homes. It may be a simple hole in the ground or something much more impressive.

Birds are champion home builders, with nests ranging from a hummingbird's thimble-sized home to the bald eagle's 3-ton giant.

Some nests can even be eaten. The cave swiftlet builds a nest from spit. It dries to a whitish color and can then be used to make a favorite Chinese dish, bird's nest soup!

Not all homes are built to last. Gorillas spend a few minutes each day making a sleeping area, and then move on the next morning.

▲ The slimiest home belongs to the parrotfish. At night it covers itself with a nest of mucus from special skin glands. The next day the parrotfish eats up the slippery mucus and swims away.

🐾 NATURE'S BEST DAM BUILDER

The American beaver is famous for building dams across rivers and streams. The beaver has four huge front teeth that can chop down a small tree in minutes. It lays the wood in the water to make the dam. When the dam is finished, a pool of water builds up behind it.

Then the beaver can make its home, called a lodge, in the pool. The living quarters in the lodge are above water level, with underwater tunnels that lead to the outside world. In the lodge a beaver family has warmth and protection in the winter.

Beavers grow up to 3 feet (80 cm) long.

▶ A beaver tows building material to its dam.

▲ Bald eagles make the biggest nests
in the bird kingdom. The largest
ever seen was 10 feet (3 m) across
and more than 20 feet (6 m) deep.

LONGEST JOURNEYS

▲ North American caribou make the longest land-animal migrations. They walk about 808 miles (1300 km) every year to summer pastures in the Arctic regions of northern Canada. After eating the new-grown plants there, the caribou walk back south. They spend the winter deep in Canadian forests.

Many animals have no fixed home. They spend their lives moving, or migrating, long distances to reach fresh food supplies or warmer climates.

Birds are the world's biggest long-distance travelers. Every year millions of them migrate around the world. Terns circle the world between the Arctic and Antarctic. Golden plovers fly 6,214 miles (10,000) km between South America and Canada. Land animals such as the caribou also migrate. The green turtle swims 1,243 miles (2000 km) to breed on an island in the Atlantic Ocean.

▶ Over its lifetime, an arctic tern may fly more than 621,400,000 miles (1 million km).

🐾 FLYING FROM POLE TO POLE

The arctic tern makes the longest migration of any animal. Terns breed in large colonies in the Arctic, when it is summer in the north. After breeding, they usually lay 1–3 eggs. The terns then fly off south, on a 12,430-mile (20,000-km) journey to Antarctica. By the time they get near Antarctica, it is summer there. The terns spend the long days fishing off the coast, where they dive for fish and other small sea creatures. As summer ends, the terns reverse their journey and head north again, ready to start another breeding season in the Arctic summer.

Arctic

Antarctica

The route of the arctic tern marked by the arrows.

Long wings are good for gliding flight.

The body grows up to 4 feet (1.25 m) long.

▲ The albatross has the longest wingspan of all birds. From tip to tip, its wings can measure over 12 feet (3.7 m).

The wandering albatross covers great distances, even though it stays mostly in southern seas. It eats squid and other sea creatures, drinks seawater, and sleeps while floating on the surface. It visits land only for breeding.

▲ Monarch butterflies leave Canada in autumn to fly more than 1,864 miles (3000 km) to sunny Mexico.

LIFE SPANS

Most animals have shorter lives than humans, but a few can outlive us. These include deep-sea tube worms and giant tortoises, both of which can live over a century.

▲ Most insects live a short while, but the colorful jewel beetle can live for about 30 years.

Few animals survive their full lifespan to die of old age. Most die young from accidents, disease, or when killed and eaten by other animals.

Even if a wild animal manages to survive into old age, this has its own dangers. For example, old elephants often starve to death because their teeth fall out and so they cannot eat properly.

But there are a few animals that live for a long time. Some researchers claim that the giant turtle of the Pacific Ocean Galapagos Islands may live for over 200 years!

◀ Killer whales are the longest-lived mammals in the sea. Females can survive up to 80 years, but males live only about 50 years.

◀ Elephants have a life span of over 60 years. They are the longest-lived land mammals, aside from humans.

▲ Goldfish belong to the long-lived carp family. The oldest on record was a pet fish called Tish. It lived for 43 years.

🐕 FROM A DAY TO A CENTURY-PLUS

Only a Day The mayfly lives for just a day or so once it reaches adulthood.

Long Jumper Most kangaroos live about 5–7 years, but the oldest on record died at 23 years.

Longest-Lived Fish The lake sturgeon can reach 80 years old.

Oldest Bird The wandering albatross can live over 70 years.

Ancient Islander The lizardlike tuatara lives on islands off New Zealand. It can survive for 100 years or more.

▶ Tortoises can live far longer than humans. The oldest on record was 152 years old when it died.

EXTREME SURVIVAL

Surviving in very hot or cold places can be tough, but many animals do. These animals have special features that allow them to lead normal lives in such extreme conditions.

▲ Siberia's tiny birch mouse survives icy winters by sleeping from early September to the following May. During its long sleep the mouse can lose about half its normal body weight of .4 ounce (12 g).

There are lots of ways to survive the cold. Many animals have thick fur, others dig holes for protection. Some escape winter altogether by finding a hole or cave, then going into a type of sleep called hibernation.

When it hibernates, an animal's breathing and heart rate become very slow. It uses much less energy and may survive all winter using the fat stored from its last meals. All sorts of animals hibernate, including hedgehogs, squirrels, bats, and toads. When they wake up in spring, they all go hunting, for they are *very* hungry!

◄ Foxes are the smallest members of the dog family. The arctic fox has thick fur, short furry ears, and fur on its footpads. This natural overcoat for protection helps it survive in temperatures far below freezing, often as low as −58°F (−50°C).

🐈 DESERT SURVIVORS

Big Drink Camels are able to survive using water from desert plants. They also drink huge amounts of water when they can, up to 13 gallons (50 L) at a time.

Below Ground Some desert frogs and toads go underground, protecting themselves in a coat of spit or mucus. When it rains, they dig themselves out again.

Stinger The desert scorpion stings its prey, crushes it, and injects a digestive fluid. The scorpion then sucks up the liquified prey. It does not need an extra water supply to survive.

The scorpion's sting is in its tail.

▲ The ice fish can survive in chilly water of 29°F (−1.5°C). It has a natural antifreeze that stops its body liquids from freezing.

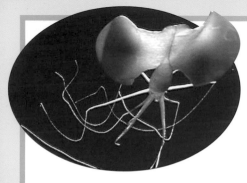

▲ The spidery squid.

ANIMAL RECORDS

Here are some facts and stories from the world of animals.

SPIDERY SQUID

In 2001 researchers found a new kind of squid, living up to 3 miles (5 km) deep in the water. The mystery beast has longer tentacles than other squids. The tentacles are also much thinner than those of a normal squid and have an elbowlike bend. Researchers think the new squid drags its spidery tentacles in the water, waiting for small sea creatures to get caught in them.

MICRO LIZARD

In 2001 a new kind of lizard was found on the island of Beata, in the Caribbean Sea. The dwarf gekko is only about a half an inch (16 mm) long, making it the smallest lizard known.

The Caribbean is also home to other tiny creatures, such as the bee hummingbird and the world's thinnest snake, the threadsnake. It is so slim that if you could take the lead out of a pencil, the threadsnake could wriggle inside the hole!

SNAKES ALIVE

The reticulated python is a huge snake. The longest ever seen was more than 33 feet (10 m).

◀ The Siberian tiger is the biggest wild cat. Adult males can weigh more than 661 pounds (300 kg).

CREEPY-CRAWLY TERROR

The most common thing for people to be frightened of is the spider, a fear called arachnophobia. Despite their appearance, most household spiders are harmless.

SLEEPY HEADS

Koalas are the champion sleepers of the animal kingdom. A koala usually spends about 22 hours a day sleeping. The slow-moving South American sloth comes in a close second, spending 18–20 hours a day asleep.

FAST FLYER

The Australian dragonfly is the speed king of the insect world, having been timed hurtling along for a few moments at 36 mph (58 km/h). Some flies and moths have been recorded flying at nearly 25 mph (40 km/h).

MINI MAMMALS

The smallest horses are called falabellas. One of these stands just 28 inches (71 cm) high at the shoulder. The pygmy white-toothed shrew is the smallest mammal of all. The tiny creature is only 2 inches (6 cm) long.

SPRINTING OSTRICH

The world's biggest bird is the ostrich, which can stand nearly 10 feet (3 m) tall. Even though it cannot fly, it is the fastest-running bird. An ostrich has been timed running across the plains of Africa at 45 mph (72 km/h), with a stride at least 2.3 feet (7 m) long!

▲ Penguins are the deepest-diving birds and can stay underwater for about 18 minutes. They live in Antarctica and fish in the icy waters there.

▼ The ostrich lays the biggest eggs. They can be 7 inches (18 cm) long and have as much yolk as 24 hens' eggs.

ANIMAL WORDS

▲ Terns flocking together before migrating south.

Here are some words used in this book that you may not know.

ANTIFREEZE (AN-tee-freez)

A liquid that has a lower freezing point than water. The ice fish has a natural antifreeze that allows it to live in icy waters without trouble.

ARCTIC (ARK-tik)

The area around the North Pole where it is cold and mostly ice-covered. The area around the South Pole is the Antarctic. Terns migrate between the poles every year.

CAMOUFLAGE (KAM-uh-flahzh)

Colors and patterns used by various animals to help them blend into their surroundings.

CARNIVORE (KAR-nuh-vor)

An animal that eats the flesh of other animals. Many carnivores eat other things, as well as meat. For example, bears enjoy gobbling up tasty berries in springtime.

▲ The eagle is a bird of prey, or raptor. This tame bird shows its sharp, hooked beak.

FLIGHTLESS BIRD (FLITELESS BURD)

A member of the bird family that has wings too small for it to fly. Examples include the penguin, the ostrich, and New Zealand's kiwi. Chickens are not quite flightless. A female has been timed in flight for a record-breaking 13 seconds.

HIBERNATION (HYE-bur-nay-shun)

A sleepy state in which some animals pass the winter—to avoid the cold and because there is not enough food to eat. An animal that hibernates lives on the fat its body stores over the summer. It uses this stored fat while it sleeps. Some animals, such as bears, don't sleep all winter. They wake from time to time and eat food stored nearby.

MAMMAL (MAM-UHL)

A warm blooded animal that feeds its babies mother's milk. Examples include bears, dogs, cats, and humans.

MIGRATION (MYE-GRA-SHUN)

The route followed each year by an animal to find warmer weather and a better food supply. Migration routes can be very long. Many birds fly thousands of miles, as do some mammals, such as the Canadian caribou, that walks to and from the Arctic.

PIGMENT (PIG-MUHNT)

Coloring material in the skin. Pigments in a chameleon's

▲ The gray whale migrates farther than any other mammal, on sea routes longer than 12,340 miles (20,000 km).

skin allow it to change color from yellow to green or brown.

PROTIST (PROH-TIST)

A simple form of life, mostly no bigger than a dot, though some protists are larger. They come in all sorts of different shapes, from jellylike blobs to things that look more like micro-mushrooms.

RAPTOR (RAP-TUR)

A bird of prey, such as an eagle. Raptors all have sharp,

hooked beaks for tearing into their prey, as well as curved claws called talons

▲ Pictured above, a tiny protist, seen through a powerful microscope.

ANIMAL PROJECTS

These experiments will help you find out more about the animals that live near your home.

There are billions of animals on our planet. Humans are outnumbered many times over, especially by creatures that are smaller than us. For example, there are likely to be many more spiders in your home than people. Take a closer look around—you may be surprised at what you find!

◀ Butterflies and spiders are common household visitors.

TAKE SOME SOIL SAMPLES

Many creatures such as tiny bugs, slithery earthworms, and multi-legged centipedes, live in the soil below your feet. In this experiment you can take a sample of soil to see what's in it.If you like, wear a pair of rubber gloves to avoid getting your hands dirty.

1. You need a garden trowel, a clean sheet of paper, and a magnifying glass. Wash and dry a glass jar to carry the soil sample, and be ready to dig several times for specimens.

◄ Here a bee moves very slowly through grass in late summer.

► Frogs love damp places in quiet corners.

ANIMALS AROUND YOU

Making a regular wildlife report is a good way to get an accurate idea of what animals live around you.

The best plan is to look at the same time, once a week (or daily if you like), then collect the notes as a monthly report.

You will soon get a good idea of what the wildlife is doing where you live.

AUGUST - ANIMALS SEEN

Birds

Thrush x2

Robin x1

Blackbird x2

Mammals

Fox x1

Badger x1

Other

Snail x8

Slug x4

Spider x6

WILDLIFE NOTES Use a notebook, and mark your creature-count in columns. One page per month should be enough room.

2. Place soil in the jar. If you see a worm, put it in the jar, but take care not to harm it.

3. Empty the soil onto the paper sheet and inspect for interesting creatures.

4. Use the magnifying glass for a closer look. Put the soil back when you have finished.

INDEX

arachnophobia 27

bat 12
bears
    brown 2
    polar 13
beaver 18
bee 12, 31
beetle 4, 22
birds 18
    albatross 21, 23
    cave swiftlet 18
    condor 8
    eagle 18, 19, 28, 29
    golden plover 20
    hummingbird 8, 18, 26
    kakapo parrot 12
    kiwi 8, 28
    ostrich 27, 28
    owl 8
    penguin 27
    peregrine falcon 9
    Spix's macaw 8
    swan 9
    swift 6
    tern 20, 28
butterflies 8, 21, 30

camel 25
camouflage 16, 17, 28
caribou 20, 29
caterpillar 7
chameleon 17, 29
cheetah 6, 7
cicada 12
cockroach 7

dog, fox, wolf 12, 15, 24
dolphin 12, 15
dragonfly 7, 27

elephant 4, 22, 23

fairy fly 8
fish
    brotulid 11
    cuttlefish 7, 17
    dwarf goby 10
    goldfish 23
    great white shark 10, 14
    ice fish 25, 28
    lake sturgeon 23
    parrotfish 18
    sailfish 6, 7
    sargassum 16
    seahorse 10
    squid 11, 26
    stonefish 11
    sturgeon 23
    whale shark 10, 11
frog, toad 25, 31

gecko lizard 7, 26
giraffe 4, 5
gorilla 18
grasshopper 7
    locust 14

hare 16
hibernation 24, 28
horse 27

kangaroo 6, 23
koala 14, 27

lion 2, 15, 29

mayfly 23
migration 20, 29
moth 8, 13, 27
mouse 24

owl 8

protist 4, 29

scorpion 25
shrew 14, 27
sloth 27
snakes
    mamba 7
    reticulated python 26
    thread 26
    vine 16
spiders 27, 30
    bird dropping 16
    goliath tarantula 5
    money 5
    patu marplesi 5

tiger 16, 26
tortoise, turtle 22, 23
tuatara 23

whales
    blue 4, 10, 11
    grey 29
    killer 15, 22

zebra 16, 29